About the Author

Alison Huckvale can usually be found planning a football training session for her own team, watching football on TV or sat in the King Power Stadium supporting Leicester City. However, writing a poetry book was always top of her to do list. She also enjoys painting and crafting. She is twenty years married to David with two very determined daughters Olivia and Holly-Mae. Bella, the family schnoddle keeps everyone on their toes, unlike 'Fred' the pet tortoise owned forty years earlier in childhood. Despite the recent sale of her beloved Camper Van, named Charlie, who spent more time hoping for travel, than travelling, Alison and her family plan to explore as many places as possible regardless of their disabilities. Who knows, one day that could even be to the beautiful Outer Hebrides she fleetingly visited for inspiration in her writing.

The Tortoise of Hope

Alison Huckvale

The Tortoise of Hope

Olympia Publishers
London

www.olympiapublishers.com
OLYMPIA PAPERBACK EDITION

A CIP catalogue record for this title is
available from the British Library.

ISBN: 978-1-78830-915-8

Portions of this book reflect the author's present recollections of
experiences over time. Some names and characteristics have been
changed, some events have been compressed, and some dialogue has
been recreated. Other names, characters, places and events are products
of the author's imagination, and any resemblances to actual events or
places or persons, living or dead, is entirely coincidental.

First Published in 2021
Tallis House
2 Tallis Street
London
EC4Y 0AB
Printed in Great Britain

Dedication

To my husband David who has always held belief and confidence
that I'd get there in the end.

Acknowledgements

I would first of all like to thank my family and friends who have shared life's journey - in times of struggle and celebration too, you all continued to share my passion and love of writing, even when I felt I didn't quite have the right words.

I have to thank Lydia Towsey - Arts in Mental Health Coordinator at Leicestershire NHS Partnership Trust for her hours of time reading and helping me draft and edit my poems, encouraging me to pursue a career as a poet and giving me inspiration in her own widely anthologised and published work.

I would like to thank all of my fellow writers at The Bradgate Writers for where I started my poetry journey. Upon admission to the Bradgate Mental Health Unit, you welcomed me to try something new, to express myself with words - I owe you endless thanks for the sessions I have been able to attend over the last four years. Listening and sharing each others work has been invaluable.

I owe huge thanks to Ian Mitchell for his illustrations, which he created from just a sample of my poems. You depicted the tortoise just as I imagined.

I am hugely grateful to Barry Green who took time to diligently read the poems from start to finish offering me his experienced eye as a writer himself.

Finally, I would like to thank the NHS staff at the Orchard Resource Centre in Hinckley, Leicestershire for giving me the services to help overcome and manage my mental health.

Chapter 1- Asleep

The Great Barker

The autumn bark spoke very little last year;
fruit forgotten, like a barrier in nature's ear.
If only it could talk of the stock and security
that was once shared, with hope and prosperity.

Safeguarding the goodness nurtured within,
is reflected in its rings of maturity, built in.
Imprinted from a seed at birth, with wavering worth,
the passion held within this great oak is unearthed.

Its size is shadowed by the source of all life,
a reflection of light, authentic to nature's strife.
Hope represented in the sight of chromatic leaves.
Next season, Great Barker, you'll grow I believe.

You'll tower in spirit, share your own fantasy tale.
An abundance of rich acorns in heavenly scale.
Quickly, we'll forget the year before last
because what's most important is now; forget the past.

Poem collaborated with Holly-Mae Huckvale (daughter aged sixteen).

White Words

Withe whitings
thew whitefaces
whet the whiteflies
whitewashed wit
hew the whiteboard
tie the whitethroat
tew white with
whitened tie
whither
white
it.

Loneliness in the Hebridean Farmhouse

The sad farmhouse shivers in damp timbers.
Stone cold walls float in moistened cement,
foundations weakening with no support forthcoming.

The vicious wind howls and knocks on rotten window panes,
but still no-one answers.
Gales break through the shutters, weakening glass
laying siege to the guttering.

Rigorous roars fail to lift the bleak house out of darkness,
as green northern lights pale against the blackened chimney stack.
On barren moorland, wind whispers to the isolated farmhouse,
solitary and desolate – "Where are my companions?"

When will the farmhouse rise from its loneliness?
The yearning log, tired of restoration?
Scared of impeding storms.
Abandonment and demise a threat;
only time will tell.

On Charge

My uncharged mobile is a quiet magpie,
a colourless chameleon,
frozen fat in a whaling iceberg.
It's a powerless dam of trapped memories,
an injured Olympian;
its strength, sapped by thirsty cacti,
wireless callers and demands.
Blackened face; reflective.
In darkness, in thought.
It's jet-lagged, actionless and hungry,
like a refrigerator craving its fill.
Conversations on hold,
till strength regained.
Locked-
Down.
Charging.

Insomnia in Control

Nobody sees my relationship with insomnia.
Sleeping with my eyes wide open,
Thoughts kidnapped by my mind.
Voices that won't shut up at night.
Ridiculous reminders out of the blue.
Neglected notions refuse to subdue;
insomnia in control.

The more I resist, the more it persists.
My mind, desperate to get out of there.
Twisting and turning, my tired eyes betrayed.
Consciously, my body's curves and edges invade.
Mistakes I fear to condone, as I lie awake.
Images and messages grind my gears.
Insomnia in control.

Empty

Crumpled and empty,
I lie in the gutter!
Abandoned so recklessly,
without thought or demise.
Open to the elements,
without a shelter or home.
I'm rustling.
I'm shaking.
I'm fatigued.
I'm flailing.
How long must I wait to be lifted free?
I'm just a lonely crisp packet,
discarded like rubbish.
Heartlessly ditched.
Hopeless.
Empty.

It's in a Box

I'm being buried
under my own silence,
as though a murderous act had been committed.
What love do I feel
as the box is prepared and the lid closed?
Into hibernation I'm admitted.
It's a waiting game now.

In contrast, my keeper has buried boxes
stuffed with stifled secrets,
with no best before date.
I doubt it was love she felt
as her thoughts were labelled and emotions trapped,
amongst her faulty subconscious programming.
For her it's a waiting game, too.

Time critical situations both in boxes,
ready to be unpacked with care.
The boxes have been our place of safety
but some of the chocolates have disappeared.
Life is a set of playing cards controlled by the jokers;
re-appearance or re-address not in our hands.
Having been boxed up, is all we can hope for.

Dreams Under Arrest

My arrested dreams
warn restless stars, spiraling
inside inner space.

My Soul Mate

... and the comforting cuddles from my soul mate.
No escape from the unique texture I've ground into my bear's fur.
... and the scent of fresh bed linen as he lies on my bed each evening.
... and his shiny, black, button nose sown back onto his withering face.
... and his broken heart removed by his grandmother,
now stored elegantly in the family bureau.
... and his floppy ears, pierced with pink wool,
keeping them firmly attached to his oval head.
... and although he appears to be ageing with time,
I do not care, for he is mine.

A Well-Spent Pound

At the age of twenty-one months, it's remarkable what brain cells can recall.
One plain, ordinary bear, who growled for a pound.

On my mother's torturous weekly shop,
mingled with frozen peas, Spam and a Mother's Pride loaf,
I sat swinging my little legs wildly from the trolley seat.
Little did she realise I had spied something
down the toy aisle and had plans of my own.

When she launched a huge, yet very plain bear on top of the groceries,
I immediately insisted on holding it - to free up some space; of course.
A destined present for her godchild or so she thought.

Money must have meant a lot forty years ago, but Gregory
was going nowhere, except home with me.
Our love for each other was reciprocal,
as were our lives to be.

He glared through the thin cellophane window; Mum clocked my intentions.
How could one relationship, without human contact, mean so much –
be cemented for so little? Dad wasn't too impressed but he was a soft touch anyway.
I fought, knowing he'd be given to me - to share in a life
that neither parent could control.

Gregory never bargained for what he got either but we were one,
sharing life's ups and downs unequivocally with an unbreakable bond, even to now.

Gregory – my greatest friend of all - a well-spent pound.

Why Did She Hide?

In isolation,
to avoid undesirable thoughts?
In limbo,
to avoid difficult interactions?
In denial,
to avoid guilt or emotional pain?
In defence,
to avoid being hurt?
In a loop,
to recall past experiences?
In silence,
to avoid disapproval and rejection?
In shame,
to disappear and become disconnected.
That's why she hid.

What Happens If ...

What happens if, when I wake up
I'm not who they expected to find?
What happens if, when I wake up
I'm not me anymore?

What changes if, when I wake up,
diamonds are found healing inside me?
What changes if, when I wake up,
those gems are ripped from my heart?

What ends if, when I wake up,
the key of curiosity is unlocked?
What ends, if when I wake up
I'm told, "I don't believe you?"

Are You a Good Dream Stealer?

Imagine if you swapped dreams with the person laying beside you.
Would they recognise any of the characters or know who is who?
Could they distinguish when and where in the dream you are?
Just beginning, introductions, decisions, in the middle, how far?

Picking up the thread of someone else's dream
is like sewing with clouds and leaving no seams.
You need to make quick decisions about what happens next,
otherwise you'll leave those involved utterly perplexed.

Take hold of the situation, just as you would any other.
Does this dream fit into anything; something similar to another?
Be creative, brave and forge a positive finish.
Not like the ones you have, that falter and diminish.

Imagine having the capacity before going to sleep,
that you can take over a dream, no matter how deep.
Consciously decide on a favourable ending
so your mind is attuned, to stop disaster trending.

Only you can decide to become an effective dream stealer.
Nobody's expecting you to change characters to healers.
Just think of the thoughts that go with the actions
and you'll find you sleep more easily, without such distractions.

A Pansy for Your Thoughts

Garden flowers are my best friends.

In my hand, I held future thoughts.
Seeds with very little to talk about;
it helped once I had planted you, though.
At least I could marvel in your potential,
though you were in no position to respond - yet.
Those 'I wonder ifs?', 'What ifs?', 'How comes?',
over and over and over again.
All you asked for was
a little watering in between.

I'd talk to you like children,
repeat the same sorry tales
and hope you would turn out different,
repeating Sutton's instructions for best results.
Nothing grew last year, despite me doing all the right things.
Maybe they didn't like my tone of voice?
Was it because I'd whispered too loud?
Did I neglect you some shade and forget
a little watering in between?

Your sprouts need to show me your fresh shoots
because I'm only interested in the now.
I focus on you throughout the day - just staring,
staring as you start to open yourself up to the world.
It never happens quickly; you are conscious of that.
I'm here for you Pansy - one sprout or maybe more.
I've been patient. I can do more, plus
a little watering in between.

Overnight, our expectations gathered pace
 - a few buds, more shoots and other pansies too.
Shared laughter and loyalty, the carnival begins.
A circus of pansies performs in the streets.
Glorious, tangerine faces with purple smirks.
Gazes so hot, my ice cream melts,
as each petal paints a delightful thought.
It was as if you were telling me jokes with
a little watering in between.

Exuberant colour reflects my minds ambition,
saturated and harmonious like a rainbow doing a limbo.
Just as you had blossomed for me, it was also time to rest.
Consider the quietening music of the carnival
as it passes through for one more year.
An explosion of seeds dispersed in your path.
What colours, what creations, what stories will be told next year, with
a little watering in between?

Condor No More!

Stood on the glass balcony, overlooking the rim,
sits a New World Vulture; the Californian condor.
Previously extinct, Earth now echoes a hymn;
Settlements floored by the Canyons rapport.

I've sheer granite cliff tops,
layered coloured stonecrops.
Tall, towering limestone walls
humbled; a vertiginous gorge.

Uniformed in black, he prepares to take flight,
a frill of plumaged feathers ruffled ready.
Underside wings triangular and patchy white,
brownish eyes, ivory billed and grey legs, steady.

I'm picturesque, grandeur,
stateliness splendour.
A majestic beauty;
crevasses so austere.

Neck flushes to reflect its emotional state as wings flap wildly,
yellow to glowing reddish-orange. Thermals maintain flight.
The enduring mystery reshapes the range of motion in its wing, mildly.
Yet graceful; new ways of flying evolve - out of sight.

I've been abandoned by nature,
masked by desert and lake.
Life's wonder, now a feature;
tourists' uptake.

Adapted for walking are his deficient, blunt talons,
Without a voice box, his hiss, grunt and growl when scavenging for carrion.
We don't build typical bird nests, we create crevasses or caves from unwanted rock.
We are not your typical condor. We are intelligent, curious and social birds.

Consider: wonder versus habitat.
Consider a Canyon versus a Condor.
      Consider beauty in both, before a preference you'll arrive at -
      The Canyon no longer with its Californian Condor.

Survival of cattle and sheep maintain the Canyons ecosystem.
Free from scavengers, only taking food as part of the natural clean up.
The oasis of waterfalls cascading and riding down the overhanging rock.
If the Californian Condor is to be no more, is the canyon alone, enough?

Forty Years Forgotten

One late winter's evening,
as dusk had just settled,
the thick, brown puddle drew
ever closer to his white, fluffy head.
Why had I dropped him?

His yellow, chequered trousers and red, polyester jumper
survived the dirt.
As he lay cold,
motionless on the farmyard floor,
amongst the noise of bleating hens and tired horses,
yet to be settled in stables close by.

Aunt came to the rescue on that memorable day.
Cleansing his arctic fur, then
reluctantly putting him in the twin tub
for a quick spin.
I'd dropped him to delay going home - to elongate my stay!

Forty years later, amongst discarded soft toys,
wedged deep at the back of the lonely attic.
In a tatty, brown box, I rediscovered my friend;
recalling the childhood adventures we had shared.

In years previous, he'd sat at the bottom of my bed,
occasionally talking about his friendship with Bill Badger.
His rigid frame domineering over other soft creatures.
His ring pull exercising chat, as the elastic wound back in.

Today, its's my turn to rescue Rupert Bear;
to repair the ring pull and give him a voice once more.
No need for him to be silenced,
just as I had been.

Hope Prevailing

What an emotional rollercoaster
of bottomless pits and ingenious mechanical contrivances;
much like a suited soldier ready for combat.
Post-Traumatic Stress Disorder overrides the thematic devices,
held inside our thoughts;
like a circus of dreams.
In the same way that 'The Smiler's' cogs were vertically challenged,
a courageous and passionate woman unleashed her own butterflies.
She lay comatose.
Why? The all-important question.

Miraculously surviving the clinical error,
she woke, but in a fearful machine.
Her mind humiliated and out of control,
nagging voices attacking her vulnerable shell.
Silent - so silent - was survival no longer the question?
Flashbacks insult her night and day,
ridiculously playing
out a series of mocking events;
as though her coffin was pre-labelled -
the end of her life destined.

Silent – so silent – thoughts are provoked and jeered in torrid nightmares.
Days, weeks and even months later – remaining disconnected from loved ones,
unable to find pleasure.
She needs time to recalibrate her brain's alarm;
moral feelings, all signs of weakness and character changes.
She needs to challenge herself
and master her own ship again.

Silent - so silent - pushed to the brink,
comparable to the Incredible Hulk
who exposes his ugly body;
clothing ripped and the temper of a wild horse unbridled,
all overtaken by the sense of futility, yet again.
Withdrawn, detached - even if she functioned before.
Where has her inner self gone?
She's no soldier but unarmored, looks exactly the same - hope prevailing.

She refused to allow the violated relationship with herself win;
with courage, the shame defrosted her heart
and the glass wall cracked too.
Distancing herself from those argumentative voices,
she deciphered and depressed the vagrant tones
until they sat, ready on the launch pad of hope.
Boredom relieved,
restlessness released,
pain lightened and relationships enriched.
Hope has prevailed - silent - so silent; PTSD discharged like a ticking time bomb.
Gone!

Spiritual Path

Alone, deep seated on the spiritual path,
abstract colour darkens as the eye closes.
A typhoon of light embraces my journey
into the wilderness of light and reflections.
Green, blue, yellow and red;
a rainbow drawing me near.
Lilac, pink, lemon and purple;
all shades worn to deepen the adventure.
A bright, white light opens the door,
on a spiritual path – evermore.

What is ...?

What is dimity?
A shade of shadow white.
What is calamine?
Dusky pink, creamed all over.
What is brassica?
Sullen violet, darkened with fear.
What is plummet?
Lashings of purple to swallow up winter.
What is radicchio?
A deep red bed rock to contain all colours.
What is dusk?
Colours prevailing sleep.
What is colour, if only a shade?
Imagine.

It's Time to Open Up

Where are the holes in
my heart-broken parachute;
too ashamed to fly?

Chapter 2 - Awake

Hibernation All Over This Year

New season arrives.
Emotions flood your body.
Time to readjust.

Waking Up

You've been away, snoozing for some time.
Let's remove your lid; bring you into your prime.
Compared to last year you've overslept;
Possibly down to the way you've been kept.
You naturally needed more time to wake,
compared to a human, a tortoise takes an age to awake.

Now there's me, who I believe they forgot!
Locked in a coma, prayers in an empty teapot.
My brain cells are either tired or too shy to be woken up.
As I wait for someone or something to pour life into my cup.
I breathe like a stopwatch: on, off, several false starts, but
it's clear I'm going nowhere. I'm staying put!

Now, if you were a ladybird, you'd be off
fluttering about, showing off!
Now, if you were a bumble bee
you'd be off, searching for pollen to make honey.
But fact, is you're a tortoise
who will wake up eventually and nose around.
Whereas I need waking up,
having discovered my body's shut down.

Hours later, still no great movement in your shoebox,
mirrored by the lack of engagement, as doctors flummox.
Only minimal disturbance in the newspaper shreds.
Hospital staff rushing round looking for beds.
Progress, in you - it looks like a tunnel is starting to form.
Yet I'm placed in a machine - a tunnel - a dream?
It's a matter of minutes rather than hours, but
this white passageway of the other side, is too extreme.

You pretty much dictate when it's your time, to be
placed under your UV lamp, in your shallow wood enclosure.
I'm in this white coffin, unsure what the next action will be.
For me, I'm fearing whether they know I'm still me.
You're ready to renounce yourself - timid movements,
smelling with your throat again - such a luxury!
I'm petrified this drowning drill of a noise prolongs.
Where, oh my god, am I? There are no belongings!

I'm so anxious to see those bubbling nostrils of yours.
I'm afraid to move an inch, in case I miss the moment.
I'm in toxic panic, I've been certified dead;
you can't appreciate what's going on in my head.
Suddenly, your eyes, like stabilisers, rest on a shallow piece of bark,
If only a key could unlock the resting shell deeper within.
My eyes are focused on the white 360 degrees around me.
I'm terrified they've decided my fate and no one I'll see.

You're only seconds away, can my patience hang out?
Is it selfish to feel that I'd be happier, knowing you've made it?
Could I be in here for perhaps hotter things - surely not?
If I'm to be fried or buried alive, at last I'll know Fred survived.

I never gave Fred a second thought from this moment on.
Such a shame, after all that anticipation and expectation.
All that I thought of was being buried alive and moving on.
I think of being buried alive in a white coffin with Fred.
I think of being cremated in a casket; button pressed by Fred.
I think of being forgotten about in the MRI machine until
I starved to death and became dehydrated, losing my life under Dr Fred.
Fred was my beloved tortoise but he sadly became a terrible thought,
that leaves me with flash backs and terrors to those final days,
which were glorious for him, but not for me.
Fred made it through that year.
So did I, but it was somewhat more difficult, let's say.

Before It Controls You

Storms shout violently.
Waves misbehave.
Clowns fail to raise laughs.
Frowns evidently shaved.
Mind-blowing, complex dramas, too angry to comprehend.
Anger so furious, wrinkles offend.
Temper breaks out.
Darkened lines incensed.
Heart animatedly beats.
All sense of purpose dispensed.
Crumpled faces reflect - the mirror of hell.
Violence swells, painful tears quell.
Spontaneous fear.
Fueled, hopeless heart.
Angered once more.
Feelings impart.

Calm Versus Anger

Calm waters; peace brings harmony on the shore.
Storms sing violently, angered like a black rainbow.
So calm, so silent – feel custard setting in a deep trifle.
No sense of purpose – but anger fights violence
- strings misunderstood, on an untuned guitar.

Birdsong silences a small crowd, yet lions roar in hunger.
As steady as a military arrow resting on a shoulder,
tears are shed out in spontaneous fear.
Calmness, heartfelt inner strength, totally unwavering
- padlocked keys bullied, fighting to break free.

It's Howling ...

When the wind gales through the weakening glass …

It's howling the ears off St. Andrews.
It's howling herberts and sherberts.
It's howling electric eels and octopi.
It's howling Harris tartan, too.

Each sound, sheer music to the ocean's lull.
It's howling black pudding and deep pies.
It's howling swollen ferries and infant cries.
But the howling maintains the Islands' identity, too.

Excuses I Might Use

Fog is suffocating my mind.
Sleep is learning a new language.
Anticipation is rousing mental chatter.
Overwhelming helplessness is the result;
surrendering stress.

The Day I Had Fun With Time

Taro's enchanted clock face blushed.
Hands swapped places.
Enthusiasm in abundance.

Dancing cogs tangoed together.
Alarm bells positioned.
Yet to be tickled by time.

I had so much time on my hands.

However, patience wasn't my forte.
All I yearned for, absent.
Daring myself an opportunity to swing.

Fresh air coasted by me.
Unnerved by the freedom presented.
Never awakening the sleeping cuckoo.

Wind whittled past the mahogany door,
insight deflected by springs,
Taut yet unsuppressed.
Heaven awakened as my pendulum swung.

Today I had fun with time,
Inside my grandmother's clock.
Minutes more, hours more;
Enchanted.

From Which Perspective?

Water damaged paper, now useless for origami.
Its image depleted, like blood without iron;
purple rain resonating in my mind.
Valuable artwork a mere imperfection;
no legible use or purpose - discarded from sight.

Attitude lends us a fresh perspective.
Judge wisely its dampened impression;
no stereotypical perception or ideological slant.
Isolated outlines, ink stains irritate prey;
conviction noted, then thrown away.

Personality 'Things'

A rainfall of words shrouds my personality,
but I'm asked to consider life in reality.
Name two things you would like to understand?
As I bury my head in lost quicksand.
It's not easy to pin down,
or put into words -
a mind broken down,
washed up or misheard.

What is personality?
What shapes personality?
The session begins,
ground rules underpinned.
Characteristics and traits developed from birth,
'things' that define your being and worth.
It's the way that you think, feel and behave.
Misgivings and notions taken to grave.

I flinch at the thought of what will come next.
Seeking out others, equally vexed?
Am I expected to join in?
Will I seem genuine?
The first slide spells it out
as if there's no doubt -
lifestyle, childhood, family and friends;
all matters I struggle … to comprehend.

Biological traits, social constraints
and 'those' psychological weights.
Ultimately, your mental health;
no lesser the mention of physical wealth.

A mixture of it all forms who you are,
just like the charismatic blend in a rare cigar.
Other professionals, what do they think?
Throw gambling, alcohol and drugs in the rink.

I sit there and consider my life - black or white;
 no in-betweens to expedite.
'She's a bit strange', I know they'll reflect;
a real weirdo – they'll probably detect.
But I won't be put off
or compared – a stand-off.
I'm just here to find out
about life's roundabout.

Persistent, pervasive and problematic symptoms.
Distressing, tormenting, anguishing phantoms.
You'll withdraw to quiet corners, rescede into yourself;
a reticent, shy loner on an inhibited bookshelf.
Often, you're labelled as emotionally unstable -
Cluster A, B or C – all plausible labels.
Let's begin - look at each one.
Before we start - any questions, anyone?

I'm nervous, I'm scared – afraid of the dark.
Will they tell me; the ball is out of the park!
I think I'm prepared to take it all in;
stand up, be brave, be a heroine.
No one will blame me if I just don't get it.
If I just can't hack it, I'll simply leg it!

Cluster A – odd and eccentric, paranoid, schizotypal,
socially and emotionally detached - like a flower's carpal.
Blunted emotions, distant, aloof,
interaction avoided, less pleasure – all proof.
Awkward, embarrassed, emotionless, inept,
gauging perception – hard to accept.

Well, I am unconventional, if that's classed as odd;
puzzling and mystifying in all likelihood.
Sporadic, suspicious and somewhat bizarre,
like a violin's fiddle playing guitar.
I'm definitely stubborn, bolshy, perverse.
OMG! Can it get worse?

Cluster B – dramatic, anti-social, emotional, erratic,
histrionic, narcissistic, ostentatious, bombastic.
Manipulative, unstable, superficial – yet grandiose.
Ultra-confidence – yet fragile; open not closed.
Abandonment feared, genetic low mood,
self-esteem a trait, you'll also allude.

Well, I am known to exaggerate minimal things,
illuminate the findings – quite satisfying.
I may have been told I manipulate others;
can't say that about sisters or brothers.
Literary forsaken, discarded, dispensed;
Let's forget all about it – set precedence.

Cluster C – anxious, fearful, uneasy, distraught,
obsessive, compulsive, avoidant in thought.
Cowardly, clingy, yearning control,
ego syntonic, not easy to cajole.
Hypersensitive and obnoxious,
apprehensive and fractious.

Well, it's easy to see which ones of these
symbolise my personality frieze -
like textures of wallpaper, sandpaper, newspaper;
scouring heights of mental skyscrapers.
I'm definitely obsessive – all consuming,
timid, faint-hearted, totally overwhelming.

It's a developmental, interpersonal disorder,
where core beliefs are put out to launder.
Defined as a pattern of inner experiences,
not a set of mere coincidences.
Behaviour's indifferent to that of what's expected,
compared to an individual's culture, reflected.

So, that's why relationships are hard to hold;
people's perceptions thus uncontrolled.
So, what therapy can I have? I ask outright.
Psychological therapies preferred, I write.
Is medication not deemed more discrete?
Popping pills – not bittersweet.

Emotions take over the ability to think.
Hyper arousal creates a collapse – doublethink!
Preconscious, imaginative, mental naivety
requires careful analysis of behaviour – toxicity.
'Recognition will define your destiny' -
'Manage my emotions, rather than them manage me'.

Empathise, be mindful; relate actions to thoughts.
Use Buddhist philosophy, constructed and taught.
Communicate well and regulate feelings,
connect emotional misunderstandings.
Understand myself, who I am and my values;
my thoughts and feelings – notwithstanding.

Learn to console others, straighten up a friend.
Use coping strategies, ready to hand.
Learn to recognise what triggers behaviour,
attend therapy sessions, mediation: a saviour.
Set limits and boundaries for yourself to adhere to -
mentalise, reflect, continue to work through.

All this in two hours; it's a lot to mop up,
sat there wishing they'd end and sum up.
I guess they've answered my questions unasked,
as I hide behind my confident mask.
Personality 'things' too many to mention.
Filing the notes in my 'Mental' collection.

Today I'm Lost for Words

Today, is one of those days,
when I can't explain how I feel,
In fear of saying it all wrong.
I can't find the words
that I'd usually find,
because today is one of those days
where my mind and mouth are in conflict;
neither one ahead of another.
Both fight to explain how I feel,
although silence is the best word of all.

Who Do We Really Trust?

I was weak so didn't tell - I decided
to keep the silence.
I was good at skirting around things.
Dressing them up, making them into something else,
resembling something similar, to avoid the truth.

I couldn't expect her to read my mind.
What a foolish, goofy, absurd, laughable suggestion.
I know this, from the words I'd been called.
What a dork, dimwit, cretin, moron and imbecile.
It had all kicked off from the year my pencil case was stolen.
Material possessions can easily be replaced, I found,
but what about the spilt ink contaminating my thoughts?
I became the donkey handing things over on demand:
starting with food then moving onto cash.
I was vulnerable but wanted to be friends,
so obliged, in return for 'hanging out' after school.

I developed my own safety mechanism - lying.
I was good at it, convincing and credible.
But all I wanted was someone to talk to.
Someone that I could trust,
in return for me being honest.

She never attempted to read my mind.
She was compassionate, considerate, patient and kind.
I poured out my anxieties, misgivings and fear.
As she listened, supported and dampened my tears.
I opened up dark passageways from my lurid past,
tore down the curtains, protecting answers asked.

My life all in pieces like a broken promise.
She helped me understand and alleviate my thoughts.
She encouraged, affirmed and bolstered my inner crust.
That's when I knew, she was the one I could trust.

If Only My Wheelchair Could Talk

From the day my wheelchair arrived,
I disappeared!
My wheelchair had the centre of attention,
but her voice came from within.

Purposely, I'd selected a chair
without any push handles.
However just the presence of a person
close by, gave my wheelchair power.

People addressed the chair or carer.
That misperception ground me down.
I can't play hopscotch no more,
but I do have a voice.

Although I felt ignored and dishonoured,
I felt as if assumptions were made.
If only my wheelchair could speak:
sound resonating through its spokes.

Awaken

Stubborn leaves littered his path;
perhaps an alternative route would be quicker?
Already moving faster than his heart beat,
after the brief acquaintance with a rat.

Slowly reemerging on his high heels -
the protective shell dips and dives,
as the clever steadfast dude,
stabilises his plastron to move.

Carrying its home and protective shelter,
he wears his skeleton inside and out.
His throat a nose, his nose a voice;
complex social behaviour, for a recluse.

On his darker side, he is dominant,
aggressive, curious, elevating his head to bite.
Whilst retiring into inactivity and depression,
withdraws head and limbs, hissing in fright.

Despite creeps, he's a solitary roamer;
carapace scutes safely camouflage.
Foraging, food fills his tender stomach
before torpor opens the door back to a safe place.

A Place for Chatter

I enjoy jubilance and celebration, laughter and times of noise,
but I also appreciate some quiet.

Not 'quiet' literally,
but a quiet that creates clear poise.

Free space:
the ability to ignore voices within our heads.
The time and effort it takes, to have that ability to switch off;
so incredibly difficult with time to face.

I tame my mind into seconds before minutes, first.
If only I had a volume control button too.
Why do they choose to talk between themselves?
It's like having loads of loose change,
in a bulging,
old purse.

It's not like I'm about to ask any questions.
Not now, when there's quiet and I'm not involved.
Otherwise I'd be creating the damn voices
in my head, as creations.

I take advantage of the silence I'm given.
Yet anxiety escalates, when a whisper from one of the voices begins.
It only needs to be a whisper and normal has gone -
if there is a 'normal' volume?

How do I address the quietness?
It's far too loud right now!
Help me! It's not a game.
I hear whispers, clicks and ear-drumming like chess.

I can't infer what he wants.
Noise escalates to royal roars and yammering insistently.
I've done something wrong.
What have I done wrong that haunts?

Can my hands address the quietness?
Can the movements of my head help?
Can I answer back, shout, scream, try and reason - what is the answer?
How can this quietness be addressed?

It's so hard, but I try and comprehend
An inner knowledge, that I can't understand,
Let alone how they fit with my thought patterns.
But I feel I'll be ruled by them in the end.

Books will tell me that I require a state of mind
that requires discipline and efforts.
Chatter isn't heard in our ears,
but as clear as day in our minds.

I can't drown out this chatter.
I'm living alongside it, where the negative thoughts continue to confuse me.
There was a confidence there: hidden courage, beliefs, wisdom and beauty.
I just need to find it from all the clutter.

Negative chatter is getting its own way. Why?
Mental chatter kicks in and asks, 'Why'?
Chatter deals on assumptions and fear.
Fear of what I hear in the future or past, but what about now?

I relapse and my inner wisdom resurfaces.
My overactive brain doesn't know when to stop.
When it's our own, mental chatter creeps in inhibited,
I should control the unwelcome nervousness.

I should reward the power of positive thoughts.
Make those mantras and affirmations count,
put those negative thoughts in specific places
and allow positive chatter, a place in free space.

Revealing the Past

My life revealed itself to me,
the day I stripped the passageway free.
Layer upon layer, paint and paper bare.
Scrapers at the ready, prepared to tear.
The first, second and third layers were just paint -
reluctant emulsion to tidy up, clean up the space.
To cover up the stains, the blemishes and marks.
The evidence in some cases - domestic sparks.
Magnolia first, light blue then deep green.
Colours intensified to cover up the scene.
My coloured past reveals everything bad.
Nothingness, boredom, lonely and sad.

A child revealed itself to me
as I began to strip the passageway free.
Patterned ladies and gents on horsebacks.
A reminder of the more robust years and smacks.
My own trust and optimism diluted like cordial.
Confidence so low, it grew progressively abnormal.
Another layer lifted, a much more delicate version of me.
Trauma and sorrow led to such naivety.
A blue banded stripe,
like a plaster I wore, when I fell off my bike.
When the wall is stripped bare, I'm finally free.

What We Need

All I need is something essential or very important.
All I need is to balance my needs with the needs of others.
All I need is to remember to take care of myself and not always worry about others.
All I need is a feeling, a feeling in a situation, but how necessary is it?
Is needing a want: something essential, a requisite, a must have?
Am I needing under an obligation or compulsion?
What if my need is only something I desire,
in the need to be something or someone different?
Other people would benefit from my need; now this is on another level.
Needing is a condition requiring supply or relief.
Needs are desired, sought after
and needed.

What do you need the most?

I'm an Alderney Hoglet!

Come visit my paradise without predators to fear.
My home, an abundance of flora and fauna to cheer.
I'm a gem of eccentric beauty and tame.
Leucistic genetics I can uniquely claim.
Classically nocturnal, washed out in looks.
My bristly grin in referenced guidebooks.

Nervously, my drawstring head balls into a curl.
Quills wound, but I'm an Alderney 'Spike Girl'.
Historically released from a Harrod's shopping bag,
yet not so famous, my poor perception I brag.
My hesitant gait always stopping to smell.
I'm the island's fabled, elusive mademoiselle.

My prickly coat a scented camouflage,
home for my head, belly and legs - a garage.
I'm like a spade curiously foraging for food,
sniffling vocals, armoured back and mind shrewd.
In arrays I get wobbly when hibernating beyond,
but what else can you expect from a typical blonde!

I Open My Eyes

I open my eyes – there's birdsong on the windowsill.
I open my eyes wider, to look beyond the mountainless hill.
I open my eyes, taking in the smell of freshly cut grass.
I open my eyes wider, to realise the bells ring to dedicate mass.
I open my eyes to the bitterness of coffee.
I open my eyes wider to the sweetness of sugar.
I open my eyes to the heaviness of the feather-down, duck duvet.
I open my eyes wider, wondering what mother is gonna' say.
I open my eyes and fear those fateful words.
I open my eyes wider – she's gettin' on my nerves!
I open my eyes - it's time to get up.
I open my eyes wider – I'm being licked by that darn pup.
Out of bed I get, all bleary-eyed.
Waking up, eyes open and wide.

Time to Change

Stop anxiety.
In the moment of solstice,
alter the pathway.

Paralysed

She tore down her imperfections, salty tears darkening her sleeves.
She had no place in the world: no spark left, no colour.
Guilt festered her mind ineffective and frozen panic harboured her limbs.
She sat in a foetal position in the corner - rocking, rocking, rocking.
Fingers – white-knuckled, clinging onto her bruised knees,
breathing laboured and false confidences increased, as she dwelt on
the fine details of her life; the big picture escaping her.
Everything had gone wrong again!
The whole world felt like it was breathing on her, as she struggled to survive.
Thoughts jumped from one thing to another,
sentences fragmented as she tried to make sense.
No matter how much she wanted help, no voice would come out.
In truth, there was simply no-one left to hear -
no-one with the capacity to respond.
Her head, a carousel of spinning blackness.
It panicked.
It ran.
It froze.
Paralysed.

The Hope Thieves

Hope is waking up without pain.
Pain that prevents me from being who I could be.
Hope is my wheelchair;
without it I cannot be anything close to who I'd like to be.
Hope is my husband.
We share disabilities to make us one whole.
Hope is my children,
who without them, nothing would have been possible at all.
Hope becomes something more,
when you allow others to help you and care for you.
Hope is a target:
a set goal that you put your mind to achieve.
Hope is a belief
that recovery for mental illnesses are possible.
Hope is an aspiration,
when two minds together can receive the pressure of one.
But then there's the Hope Thieves.
If pain is stolen, then I'm happy it's gone.
If my wheelchair is broken, I'll just borrow another one.
If my husband and children are ill, I'll sit by them until they get better.
But if my target is taken, I have nothing to aim for.
If I lose belief, I become depressed and ill.
If I lose all aspiration, I become isolated and numb.
So, of the many 'acts' that can be stolen,
it's down to me.
'The Hope Thieves can have none'.

Gathered in the Hood

My wheelchair and I gather in the hood each week to write.
New territory, new gang, new poetry.
Anxious and uncertain of myself, just like the rest.
We all observe the engagement between each other,
braving opportunities to chip in with a response.
Not always verbal, but a nod or shake of the head.
Complicated lives inside us, look out for each other,
acknowledging everyone is a hero in their own story.
Attempting to appreciate the life in the living of others.

Lettuce all Gone!

Watching my tortoise gnaw a piece of lettuce,
is akin to giving a title to a freshly written poem.
So, when it's gone,
let us pray.

Spring is the Best.

Some say summer is the best season of the year,
but I say not.
It all depends where you are;
it may not be hot.

Springtime is a reminder
of new beginnings.
Not like autumn,
when leaves shed endings.

New flowers bloom, new born lambs and the start of warmer weather.
As opposed to wilting flowers
from too much sun and very little rain.
Both necessities to bring new life again.

Bulbs aplenty,
flowerbeds full.
Spring's a time of enjoyment,
bright not dull.

New life is given and fresh starts can begin,
whereas the end of summer means autumn's akin.
Spring is bouncy,
summer is here,
autumn is coming,
winter provokes fear.
So, spring is the best,
naked or dressed.

Elasticity impinged.
I'm taken for a ride.
I'm erratic.
Soul awakened.

Being Normal Without an Apology

We are born as 'perfect' human beings;
perfect in every single way.
Then, over time we just become 'normal'.
We behave like most normal people
until we are addressed as weird,
different and a multitude of other things.

She remembered being told, 'You were a difficult baby',
So, she was clearly not perfect or normal.
She'd had a troubled childhood with
little happiness and expectation.
Her teenager years were overshadowed
by grief, jealousy and confusion.
During adolescence, she spent years alone,
siphoning the anxiety she'd consumed.
Through late education, she studied.
Which ladder to climb or to be 'normal'?
Later, she met the man of her dreams
after choosing a special offer in a magazine.
Marriage, work and setting up home,
all choices of their own doing.
One of the two became ill.
Everything changed;
they were outside the box now.
They're no longer the normal, married couple
with a house, a car and a job each.
It's worse - it's a life-changing health issue.
There's so much more to think about - money!
Out of the trenches they managed,
they cut back and cultivated a realistic 'normal'.

Just like any other couple in life,
moving house was all part of the routine.
Next, their first daughter came along;
she was perfect of course and they were happy.
The three of them in a lovely little family.
Some relationships are better prepared
to cope than others - I say this was.
Life was never conflict-free or effortless,
but with dedicated practices, they survived,
by rewiring and rerouting the road ahead.
Different was their uniform, unique to them.
By the time daughter number two arrived,
they kissed the comparisons of life's journey.
They were pretty much as close to normal again,
until the second of the two became ill.
Already prepared by life-changing journeys, this
was no different - so changes were made.
Another house change, adaptions at work and a lengthy
personal injury claim, but
they never, ever complained.
Two adults, two wheelchairs,
two young carers and two fish.
They grew in acceptance of paradox.
They were powerless to change
but despite places of darkness,
this family came through, with friends
acknowledging they were being normal
without an apology.

My Buoyant Soul

Harboured tight between flattened boxes,
gulping compressed air,
I am teased from lofty manifold beams.
My puncture patches itch, as I'm drawn against the loft lid.
My disguised heart burping,
shuddering to recuperate.
I'm lifted free.
Soul free.

My blood-energised bonnet is humiliated,
engulfed in violence.
You pester my inflated, dominant pod,
exacerbating my invisibility for all to see.
Whimpering inside my translucent greenhouse,
the ingredients are sabotaged.
I'm fractured.
Soul exposed.

Shower me a rainbow, nothing more than scarlet gloss.
You vent anger through bottomed lips,
quickly deflated with a kiss.
Teased imperfections,
anxious in existence.
I'm nothing more than a naked space hopper.
I'm awakened.
Soul ripened.

Irresistible high spirits, radiant, red, featured tattoos.
Charismatic, animated and buoyantly happy.
Peppiness tempered.
Pulse palpitating.

It Was the End of Summer

The remaining sun cream was returned to the bathroom cabinet.
The children returned to school,
photographs of holiday destinations ceased to be taken,
strawberries and cream teas were no more.
Deckchairs were tidily packed away until next year,
flowers stopped blooming and needed weeding ready for winter.
Warm clothes were adorned,
the whole prospect of winter loomed heavily;
the bees began to disappear,
cool winds started to re-appear.
Children playing in nearby parks lessened
and the ice-cream vendors were gone.

Chapter 3 - Alive

To Betty

Unmistakable love between two soul mates,
respecting the wishes and desires of each other.
A time for unique harmony between a pair of generous hands;
giving and sharing support endlessly.
You both developed an eternal friendship,
maturity beyond your years.
A loyal relationship transcended from a casual, yet faithful partnership.
Your enduring love was faultless.

It's a Gift

My shell is a library
translated by anxiety.
I'm not broken.
I recognise the hurt.
It's a gift.

Am I Serious?

I'm serious.
I'm stony.
I'm poker-faced glum.

I'm consequential.
I'm stark.
I'm everyone's chum.

I'm determined.
I'm committed.
I'm momentous and brave.

I'm important.
I'm significant.
I'm far-reaching and grave.

I'm wholehearted.
I'm scholarly.
I'm resolute deep.

I'm earnest.
I'm stern.
I'm anything but cheap.

I'm decidedly sombre.
I'm solemnly fierce.
I'm functionally severe.

I'm more serious than arctic.
More sarcastic than scathing.
I'm just critically austere.

A-Z 'As'pects of Hope

Fashion me a word – HOPE. An utterance as
a pause on the face of a porcelain doll.
She is bound by silence, like delicate ballerinas
gesture and posture, telling the tale.
A poetic verse littered with caesuras,
in metered composition; haemorrhaging birth.
Unspoken secrets deflate hope into dilemmas -
problems seemingly incapable of solutions.
Report odds and ends - unspecified etceteras.
The hope of continuation yet to be spoken.
She renounces 'said' words like prepared formulas;
a list of ingredients with which something is made.
Will her story stick, like textured granolas?
Promises made, undertaking oath and bond.
Hope travels behind the voice of her exhaling harmonicas. Music played
to quell her own painful silences.
Yet the sound's an emblem, hope - decorated insignias
pitched perfectly, for passers-by to throw her change.
Thoughts pass to the fruit-flowering quince japonicas,
hope cultivated in its fragrant rose-like blossoms.
If only hope could taste like pineapple karatas.
Taste-buds alert and tropical beaches yearned.
She imagines soft sand, coral reef cut off by lagunas,
freshwater pools trickle back only memories.
Hope affirmations quoted like mantras,
meaningful promises or assurances maybe.
Perhaps a story or novel, unbiographed novellas,
extended fictional work with pointed plots in prose.
Musical symbols and stanzas for orchestras
to perform, ensemble music in music hall.

Can hope remove all those illogical fears? Phobias,
discussion and conversation avoided at cost.
Hope can play a proportional part - Latin quotas
not able to form agreement or affirmation yet.
But a unique heart trapped without any replicas,
accounts of the truth wrapped tightly inside.
Complicated word patterns build in her schema,
mental codification of complex stimuli.
Phonetic components are like diamonds in tiaras,
worn by the angels for whom hope is born.
Ideal perfection is sought in imaginary utopias
where hopes and dreams can be symbolised.
A pleasing view - sweeping lawns and landscaped vistas.
Situations envisaged through listless possibilities.
Hope isn't a preamble with a contrasting 'whereas',
but a feeling, an expectation or desire for the best.
Words are swords, brave on the crest of a wave – Xiphias,
plucked from the ocean to cut down woody yuccas.
Now just look up to the constellation star Zetas
and HOPE.

Glorious Visual Treasure

Hidden behind the frozen fir tree,
glorious visual treasure.
Cannons and barrels blooming
like flowerpots in a crazed garden,
as wheelbarrows aspire to a military tattoo.
A gigantic sow races like a formidable sports car,
to come first in a pig-kissing contest.
Winning a key to the world.

Things Faster Than a Tortoise

Crabs meander frantically across the seashore.
Hares race towards a finishing post.
A blender chops vegetables quicker than a naked chef.
Flying turtles breathe faster underwater.
Can the candle wick be crocheted any shorter?

Its hard shell is like a rabbit hutch,
quickly rising higher like buildings out of mud.
Pens writing aimlessly to make sense of what is 'fast'?
Too late for the tortoise.
All has gone past.

What the Tortoise Taught Us

A tortoise is a turtle
but a turtle is not a tortoise.
Tortoises are land animals.
Turtles are amphibious.
Taught and tort.
Not-tor-tos.

I Know I'm Ready to Sleep …

When I've exhausted all the vacuuming, room to room.
When the bristles are shortening on father's broom.
When I've dusted the house from top to bottom.
When I've cut back the shrubs, ready for autumn.
When I feel my eyes closing, watching the late news.
When I've had my fill of gin and similar booze.
When I've tried to crochet and it's still no clearer and
when I know midnight is drawing, ever nearer.

A Tortoise with Purpose

"Good morning," said the hare to the tortoise,
"fancy a race from here up to the fortress?"
"Don't be silly!' responded the reclusive tortoise,
"that hill ahead is absolutely enormous."
"Well, just take your time!" replied the hare, all mysterious.
"It's obvious you'll win, what's the point? asked tortoise.
"You beat me last time, so I need to win now - obvious!"
"If you're going to win, the whole race is pointless!"
"Not to a hare, who's suffering from jaundice!"
"Oh, dear hare, I had no idea! Is it infectious?"
"Why do you ask if you're not going to race us?"
Out of curiosity, the tortoise felt spontaneous.
"Okay, let's race, if not just for the hell of it!"

Both animals set off, hare the more nervous,
running at pace, running continuous.
The tortoise stopped to snooze at the cactus.
"What are you doing?" enquired hare, all serious.
"Taking a rest, to pray - I'm religious."
"Praying won't help you, ridiculous tortoise."
"I know, but a passing bus is due shortish!"
"That's cheating, that's cheating," hare echoed in chorus.
"You didn't set any rules out of all sense of purpose,"
uttered the clever, misinterpreted tortoise.
"You'll be waiting for ages!" declared hare, furious.
"See you at the top!" squeaked the stubborn tortoise.

The confident hare arrived at the top of the fortress.
No sign or sense of the committed tortoise.
Hare waited two hours. "He's obviously not passed us."
Hare skipped back down, still no sign of tortoise.
Days past and hare's wisdom seemed utterly flawless.
"Where on earth, is that ill-mannered, arrogant tortoise?"
"I've been up and down several times; did you see us?"
shouted the tortoise, passing in his yellow Lotus.
"You're having a laugh!" cried hare, quite precocious.
"So what! My wheels cured my rigour mortis."

Connecting to a New 'Normal'

Every day seems worse than the day before.
Face-to-face contact with friends is no more.
Information spreading as quick as the virus.
No rushing around; a strange stillness within us.

We've withdrawn from each other;
to love each other, depend on one another.
The weak and the strong.
The old and the young.

In most tragedies, there is always hope,
where there are people willing to cope.
Spatially, everything has changed.
Mentally, our minds rearranged.

It's like a leaking dam,
media feeding us news jam.
Coronavirus all of the time,
self-isolating or imposed quarantine.

We're reminded of our differences,
keep going to make sacrifices.
A changed sense of what is important.
Seeing social places to meet, all dormant.

Postponed sports seasons and cancelled major events.
Poorer nations, hotels offered for the homeless, not tents.
Quarantine differentiates the rich and the poor,
yet a sudden and profound change is possible for all.

Epic acts of courage and citizenship clear,
in neighbourhoods, staying at home to conquer the fear.
Be determined to stay strong and hope maintained,
like a storm that subsides and the air washed clean.

Life before Covid19 was also a catastrophe.
Environmentally, the climate and the obscenity of inequality.
In a horrifying manner, we've abused what's natural.
We must return to a world, connected - a new 'normal'.

We must realise that we all share this earth
and it's our common interest to take care of it together.
Become less attached to the small things in life.
Work through menial conflict and petty, daily strife.

Our sense of belonging will have changed,
appreciating the face-to-face contact range.
Yes. Carbon emissions will have plummeted.
Enough food, clothes, shelter and healthcare for all.

Most people will recover, acceptance for the future.
Looking at life as art - a new picture.
Now strengthening the case for climate action
with hope, vigour, pride and satisfaction.

When we are no longer isolating, will we change?

The Persistent Puffin

Clifftops bedecked with wildflowers; rugged and remote,
greet the charismatic seabirds in breeding dress.
Existing rooftops order a spring clean,
whilst reminiscing lost mates, caught in fishing nets.
Duty dictates that he defends his burrow,
Chaplin-like, whilst new pairs browse.
Tails raised, intruders beckoned closer
for broadside billing, in-between soil showers.

Continuing the courtship, female's submerged in open sea,
eager males raft and rendezvous back to the vegetated cliff.
Cartwheeling and turning, the sea parrots parade
before clumsily landing their undercarriage.
Quickly recovering both posture and pose,
now hunkered down by windy conditions,
the feathered dinner jackets guard with white handkerchieves;
magnifying barely-vocal, raucous projections.

On the uninhabited isle, nesting material is gathered,
in an orange bill with a cornified cere.
Wings flexed, propel the rotund seabird air bound
back to the auks' incubated egg.
From a single, white elliptical wonder appears a young puffling. -
A dark powder puff in a public show ground
amongst thousands of others, colonised in parental harmony;
until winter extracts their flight feathers.

Comical faces left with little than pep-talk again,
before grounding keeps them on guard once more.
Spring grows them new jackets with darkened tail feathers,
whilst young chicks continue to heavily-populate dense nests.

Congregating in clubs on grassy knolls, gives a nutritious base
for underwater flight, to feed with little resistance.
Once puffins have dispersed, impossible to census.
Only cooler seas will keep populations persistent.

Gardens of Beauty

Penned in by the summer's breeze,
waiting patiently for flowers to bloom.
Humidity draws out the perfect petals,
singing in beautiful harmony.

Gardens decorated with terracotta tubs,
filled to the brim with plentiful primroses
as they dance and exchange pollen
with bountiful bumble bees.

A cocktail of pansies rests near the hawthorns,
merging colours from purple to tangerine.
Our garden of beauty
– an impressive spectacle seen.

'Hope' Defines Me

'Hope' was a fragile seed,
planted with unexpected results.
'Hope' discovered in unusual circumstances,
when pain crippled my tender stomach.
An ectopic pregnancy suspected but saved,
by a can of Coke and a Mars bar.
An operation suspended until morning
and a scan revealing 'Hope', in an early pregnancy.
No answers for my suffering pain,
I was discharged home to blossom.

'Hope' danced through the following weeks,
confident against all odds that I could carry.
I was on a magic carpet of newfound adventure.
All of a sudden, I was faced
with an inner silence of calm, fueling 'Hope'.
I accepted the rainbow of emotions that followed.
As the due date neared, the constant itch harboured
Fear, as there was no way I was having a natural birth.
I had maintained this stance from stage dot
and everyone knew boundaries would not be crossed.

I took responsibility before the balloon burst,
that feeling of 'Hope' realising newness and change.
I embraced those hard-to-say words from disbelievers.
I had accepted it had been okay to get things wrong,
but that I didn't have to accept other people's opinions either.
'Hope' was born into a paradoxical world of calm and chaos,
into an abundance of love and support,
amid a tasty dose of discomfort and drama.
My love for 'Hope' was all-consuming and often blinding.
No longer a fantasy, but pure, poignant as well as life-affirming.

The Special One

When I look in the mirror, I see anger, failure and guilt.
When other people look at me, they see my true self.
But hidden from the world is my inner pain.
It wasn't until someone special came,
not beside me looking into the mirror,
but looking back at me.
She changed my sorrow for joy,
she reversed hurt to happiness
and she restored kindness from pain.
I felt alive, animated and energised.
I'm free, thanks to that someone special.
Thanks, because she told me to smile.
Thanks, because she was looking out for me.
She knows me well, the real me
and she knew what I wanted to know.
That someone had just saved my life.
That special one was me -
my reflection.

As I Watched …

As I watched from above
tears fretted through the maze of freckles,
each one taking a different route
before taking a deep dive from chin to floor.

As I watched from afar,
silent anguish refused to make a fuss.
Her tormented body, visibly untroubled.
Yet inside, distressed and bothered beyond belief.

As I watched from a distance
her wrinkles reflected her visible anxiety,
as though her heart had been ripped out
and forgotten; until tears fretted once more.

Mainly a Lion

I'm a maneless lion,
lying still, surveying prey.
Bald like spaghetti
without its tangy sauce.
I am an orange, ready to peel,
thinking deeply about my heritage.
Gnawed like a half-chewed bone,
broken into by a set of false teeth.
I am harmless, yet disfigured
like a goblin's face.

You are motionless
like a curious cockroach,
watching insects fly between your eyes.
Your streams of consciousness are interrupted
like a tortoise giving birth.
You are proud, open and courageous.
You are without a mane;
a lion living in physical pain.

I am bound
like an apricot swiss roll,
mixed ingredients trapped between nature.
I am complete
like a headless statue,
asking nurture to strengthen my soul.
I am different to my ancestors,
yet unique to my pride.

You are tainted by the love of God;
growing old and setting standards.
You are my prize
amongst all odds.
Not a goldfish or a bowl.
You are orange in colour -
as honest as the wind.
You are my maneless lion,
surrounded by friends.

A Summer Ruba'i

Last year's dismal trend is ready for the Summer Car Boot;
hoping to swap or sells goods, to buy a new swimsuit.
To accommodate the new hot tub I need to be in fashion,
before I can lay back, relax and drink champers from a flute.

Take the Biscuit

Bureaucratic, tea-dunked digestives
openly submerged in a hot drink.
Packaging laid bare to greedy fingers
- iced, creamed, chocolate, silk.
Companions among many
bridging gaps to stave hunger.
Texture, flavour-enriched
crumbs mimicking the sugar.
Chocolate face-down or
chocolate face-up?
Tastebuds twitter a debate
within my china teacup.
Balancing on my thumb,
liquid chocolate spills a final time.
I take the biscuit
and demolish the whole packet.
Packaging laid empty to greedy lips
I just needed a biscuit in between sips.
No more biscuits ready to consume.
Never mind, there'll be another tearoom.

Forever Teaching

A welcome line stands at your door:
lunch boxes filled, smiles galore.
Register taken, books handed out.
Who's going to assembly? Latecomers - no doubt.

Questions posed, understanding tested.
Workbooks completed, toilet trips requested.
Next lessons starts where others finish;
all in the hope the children will flourish.

English, Maths, Science and Geography,
Computing, Art, Music and History.
Design, PE, French - all mandatory.
Handwriting and RE both ancillary.

We educate, we tutor,
we coach, we guide.
We mentor, we lecture,
we instruct, we provide.
Our role is defined.
Their future refined.

Poem collaborated with Olivia Hope Huckvale (daughter aged 21)

Precious Senses

Christened to reflect peace and tranquility,
an acorn: a name to be used throughout life.
Scent resembled a flowering water lily,
as the biblical water was poured.
A silver tree pendant warmly embraced,
to remind us from where trees grow - an acorn.

Reaching out for inspiration,
creativity rests upon others' shoulders.
Memories grow as more branches form,
developing maturity, as our brain absorbs.
More acorns are formed for lives thereafter,
awaiting comforting hands once more.

What is Recovery?

Being healthy isn't black or white;
just crowded grey shadows in the dark.
A complex network of diversions and derailments -
Signals, ready to ignite.

Fingerprint proteins under attack
like the virulence of a pathogen.
Each nerve ending akin to its passenger,
travelling north to avoid setback.

You've hit the buffers,
ran out of steam,
your link and pin fatigued -
a blaspheming bloodstream.

Immunity struggling for linear space.
An innate inspection - a detailed survey required.
Uncouple the troubled carriage,
loosen bolts in your wheelbase.

Your body fights hard to recover, heal and be cured.
Focus on what can be controlled and improved.
Find ways to accept the things you cannot change.
One step at a time, like a chess move.

Not so much a question of why, but when?
Conscious efforts, a glimpse of open fields -
Reorientated, your locomotive journey begins.
Recovery a mere phenomenon.

Lighten the Load in Episodes

The heavy-weight jacket she bears,
cripples overwhelming emotions;
only ever temporary relief
until the next episode.
Exposed. Traumatic.
Distractions in belief
and bitter punches, but
she will learn.
She will cope.

Mentally Free

Her mental castle
Understanding of her self
Towers confidence

Twisted Tortoise

Tories sit to roost
Sore torso roots
Risotto ties
Tries rot
Riots!

Rise otters
To stir or test
Trio tiers
Store set
Tote!

What it's Like to Fret

Fret is a word I wouldn't normally use;
too much like pet and not enough fear.
It has numerous meanings I'll not abuse,
but fret appears in my journey so I'm using it here.

I fretted when I first lost sight
of my mother in the supermarket, aged four.
She'd become anxious, turned a grey shade of white
whilst I was playing in Tesco's revolving door.

She fretted the next time we went out to shop.
I was too young to understand any risks.
Anxious lines on her face visibly seemed to swap
as I located the aisle, for my favourite crisps.

Her fretting became a more constant thing,
never mind where or when I went with her.
I struggled to sleep, allowed my mother to sing.
But truth be told, it was much of a blur.

I started to fret when mother left me alone.
Perhaps she now understood how to let go.
I began to appreciate the concern she had shown
but now, I felt all the worry and sorrow.

I was growing up fast, I fretted about Gran's health.
Ninety next week, never a complaint or mope,
whilst brothers and sisters had eyes on new wealth.
Unperturbed by their greed, she left them to hope.

In essence, to fret is to worry about oneself
or to agonise, stress over someone else.
We complain, make a fuss, whine and stew.
We pother, rattle and let things eat away at us, too.

The Tortoise (In the Style of James Wright 1963)

There is this shell:
an oracle of mysterious codes,
that only I can understand:
a reflection, a patience,
a journey foretelling the future.
When I take to my shell,
my head seeks wisdom.

Hope is the Healer

Life can be painful:
Suffering and misfortune.
Hope is the healer.

How I Coped, Watering my Thoughts with Hope

It wasn't easy, discovering which thoughts to bury;
talking about the memories in my own library.
But I coped by watering my thoughts with hope,
just as a circus acrobat balances on a tightrope.
We all need a safety net in some fashion.
All I needed was someone to listen, with compassion.

She took one thought and allowed it to be rained upon,
even if weeds start choking the roots I walk on.
Carefully, she teased out the worries and unpicked my thoughts,
accepting that some needed more water, earth of sorts.
Together we untangled my fear, got rid of predator voices,
addressed overwhelming thoughts, incapable of making choices.
We combated the dread of whether I'd ever stand alone,
with my trusted personal and private history, finally known.

We shared sunshine and hope, when I conquered self-worth,
by shedding light for why I felt shame on this earth.
We exhausted the 'why' when unexpected waves came;
justifying how I'd always taken the blame.
Eventually, she spread some goodness where I felt naked,
leaving me spirited, confident and more motivated.
She took hope from me as I blossomed with time,
challenging my thoughts - no longer a pantomime.

I Hate Walking to School on my Own

My school mustard jumper's hidden in my bag
to cover up bleeding wounds, just in case.
I walk through the park, inevitability known.
When I'm stripped of my coat and blazer,
hands held behind me, pushed head-first into the hedge;
so deep, down at the bottom where I am wedged.

They've taken my bag and flung it away.
They've taken my clothes and walked all over them.
They've pushed me back into the hedge as I retreat.
They've rebounded me into the opposite hedge.
They've made sure I'm scratched and said, "I'm sorry".
They've made me apologise for making them late.

Every day, except Thursday, is the same.
They both stare, sit, smirk and wait,
knowing it's my only way through.
There's no point shouting, screaming or crying.
I've tried that before and it made matters worse,
so all I do, is accept it and almost rehearse.

Usually, minor cuts heal on their own.
I'm about to tell them something I might regret.
"I hate walking to school on my own."
It had taken me weeks to rehearse this.
I feared their response: 'Why?',
knowing I couldn't answer it.

Our 1930's Holiday Camp

We pack our refined Crossley car trunk,
ready to escape from busy, daily life.
Butlins on a budget, here we come!
A week of play, with pay!
We approach the art deco facade in stepped pyramid style,
where we're welcomed by a uniformed doorman.
"Hi-de-Hi!"
"Good-day!"

As the soft lights dim in the ballroom
on the copious, chrome-plated decor,
beams bounce over the tubular steel furniture.
Oh, how the sweet music sounds
as the resident orchestra sets its tempo.
Dreamy dancers waltz with rhythm and melody;
all thoughts of home life
forgotten - for now.

For the non-energetic campers there's a whist drive too;
taking preference over billiards and ping-pong.
But we prefer the boxing tournament,
'the lure of a ring'.
Fellow campers are competing to win a week away.
Wait! Final bout is called -
right hook, left swing.
Who will stay?

Entertainment is plentiful in the outdoor pools.
Cascades of Red Coats offering a 'jolly up'.
Our week has been a total triumph.
We have danced our socks off,
sang our hearts out
and played our best hand.
"Ho-de-Ho!"
"Goodnight."

Shared Dreams

He intercepts my dream at the point I fall,
negativity weakening threads before I call.
Her mind attempts to repair weak seams,
sleep rhythms adjusted in her dreams.

He intercepts my dream at the point I jump,
winding down time - hearty body clock thump,
My insomnia now back on track.
Sleep rhythms fearing capture are back.

He intercepts my dream at the point I wake,
both replacing energy that our minds make.
An hourglass timer mimics the ultimate surrender,
when you discover shared dreams, in life to remember.

The Final Curtain

The curtain hides her; a limp barrier enveloping pain.
Privacy like elastic and diseased in the drapes.
We joke about any confidentiality warning
as I sit by her side supporting her needs.
Waiting for news - any will do.
Is it fair?

Eyes sore; her salty tears fall like intermittent rain.
Her emotions throb, ache and perspire.
The two tone, high pitched monitors cry in tune
with her anxious breaths for fresh air
All the dull beeping resonates like audio wallpaper;
her mind conditioned to the Hospital white noise.
Is it fair?

One swoosh after another an artificial wall is created
away from prying eyes, yet conscious others can't help but listen in.
Psychologically we accept the disposable cubicle, yet
continue discussions we would never ordinarily share.
How can it be that others know more than our family at times?
She is stranded yet safe in the sterile security where
Modesty is offered at least.
Is it fair?

Diagnosis laid bare; she looks up, to me and back
Digesting the doctors words and advice
Nurses hold her hand at night to calm her down
Comforting thoughts offered from other patients
find there way into the seams of the curtains as they are drawn.
But this time they block out light when its night.
Surely this is the best use of a curtain.
It is fair.

Collaborated with David Huckvale (husband) November 2019